Copyright © 2024 Milan Sostaric

All rights reserved

Copyright Notice:
© [2024] by Milan Sostaric. All rights reserved. This eBook is copyrighted material protected under international copyright laws. The copyright notice must appear on all copies.

License Notes:
This eBook is licensed for your personal enjoyment only. This eBook may not be re-sold or given away to other people. If you would like to share this book with another person, please purchase an additional copy for each recipient. If you're reading this book and did not purchase it, or it was not purchased for your use only, then please return to your favorite eBook retailer and purchase your own copy. Thank you for respecting the hard work of this author.

Disclaimer:
The information contained in this eBook is provided 'as is' without warranty of any kind. The entire risk as to the results and the performance of the information is assumed by the user, and in no event shall Milan Sostaric be liable for any consequential, incidental, or direct damages suffered in the course of using the information in this book.

Modifications:
No part of this eBook may be reproduced or transmitted in any form or by any means, electronic or mechanical, including photocopying, recording, or by any information storage and retrieval system, without written permission from the author, except for the inclusion of brief quotations in a review.

Author Attribution:
Milan Sostaric is the sole author of this work and retains all rights to it. The author holds exclusive rights to distribute, publish, and sell this eBook.

Governing Law:
This eBook and any disputes or claims arising out of or in connection with it are governed by and construed in accordance with the laws of the country in which the author resides.

Table of Contents

1. Introduction

Overview of Selling on eBay

Importance of Staying Updated and Adapting Strategies

2. Crafting High-Converting eBay Listings

Headline Magic

Why Your Title Makes or Breaks Your Listing

Crafting Keyword-Rich Titles

Examples of Winning eBay Titles

Description Powerhouse

The Elements of a Powerful Description

Using High-Quality Images to Enhance Listings

Incorporating Videos and Other Media

Call to Action Prowess

What Makes an Effective Call to Action

Crafting Clear and Concise Calls to Action

3. Pricing Strategies

Tools and Techniques for Competitive Pricing Analysis

Setting the Right Price

Deciding When to Use "Auction" Versus "Buy It Now"

Monitoring Sales Data to Understand Pricing Effectiveness

Tips for Adjusting Prices Dynamically to Maximize Sales

4. Policies and Customer Service

Detailed Descriptions and Transparent Policies

Establishing Trust Through Comprehensive Product Descriptions

Setting Clear and Fair Return Policies

5. Promotions and Marketing

Effective Use of eBay Promotions

Leveraging Social Media and Online Marketing

Email Marketing Strategies for eBay Sellers

6. Managing eBay Sales

Fulfillment Strategies

Handling Returns and Customer Complaints

Using Feedback Constructively

7. Advanced eBay Tools and Services

Utilizing eBay's Seller Tools

Exploring Third-Party Tools for eBay Sellers

Integration with Other E-commerce Platforms

8. Staying Competitive on eBay

Monitoring eBay's Changing Algorithms and Buyer Preferences

Strategies for Staying Updated with eBay's Changes

Encouragement to Continuously Test and Refine Listing Strategies

9. Conclusion

Recap of Key Strategies

Final Thoughts and Best Practices for eBay Selling

10. Appendices

Checklist for High-Converting eBay Listings

Glossary of Terms

Additional Resources

INTRODUCTION

In the fast-paced and competitive world of eBay, standing out is not just an advantage—it's a necessity. This eBook is designed to transform your eBay listings into highly persuasive, high-converting sales pitches. From crafting magnetic headlines to creating compelling calls to action, each chapter of this guide will provide you with actionable strategies to attract buyers and increase sales.

CHAPTER 1: HEADLINE MAGIC

Why Your Title Makes or Breaks Your Listing

The first impression is crucial in almost every aspect of life, and the world of eCommerce is no exception. On platforms like eBay, where countless listings vie for attention, the title of your listing acts as the frontline ambassador for your product. It's not just a label; it's a potential buyer's first point of contact with your offering. The effectiveness of your title can determine whether a buyer clicks on your listing or scrolls past it.

A well-crafted title serves multiple functions:

- **Attracts Attention:** It stands out amidst a sea of competitors.
- **Delivers Information:** It quickly informs the buyer what the product is.
- **Incorporates Keywords:** It is optimized for search both within eBay and external search engines like Google.
- **Invokes Curiosity:** It makes the buyer want to learn more about the product.

Given the limited space and immense importance of this component, mastering the art of title creation is essential for any successful eBay seller.

Learn How to Use the First 80 Characters to Make Your Listing Pop

The initial 80 characters of your title are arguably the most critical — this is what buyers see first and what is often displayed in search results, emails, and mobile views. Here's how you can make the most of these characters:

1. **Start with Primary Keywords:** Identify the most important keywords that potential buyers are likely to search for. Use tools like Google Keyword Planner or eBay's own search bar to understand popular search terms related to your product. For instance, if you're selling a vintage watch, key phrases might include "vintage," "antique," "watch," and specific brand names or models.

2. **Be Specific and Descriptive:** General titles get lost in the shuffle. Specify important attributes that are likely to catch a buyer's attention or answer a critical question. Include model numbers, brand names, specific colors, or unique features that set your product apart. For example, "Vintage Rolex Submariner 1970 Blue Dial" is much more compelling and informative than "Old Men's Watch."

3. **Use Natural Language with Keywords:** While it's important to include keywords for SEO purposes, your title should also be easy to read for actual humans. Balance keyword usage with natural phrasing. Overstuffing your title with keywords can make it confusing and may even hurt your search rankings due to perceived spamminess.

4. **Highlight Unique Selling Points (USPs):** If your product has a particular selling point that distinguishes it from similar items, make sure it's included in the title. This could be anything from "unopened" or "brand new" to "limited edition" or "rare."

5. **Create Urgency or Scarcity:** Whenever applicable, words like "last," "only," or "rare" can create a sense of urgency or scarcity, encouraging quicker decision-making from potential buyers.

6. **Avoid Jargon and Unnecessary Abbreviations:** While certain abbreviations are common and understood in specific categories (like NWT for "New With Tags"), avoid overly technical jargon or obscure abbreviations that might confuse buyers.

By strategically using the first 80 characters of your eBay title, you can dramatically increase the visibility and attractiveness of your listings. Remember, the goal is not just to inform but to entice. A buyer's journey often begins with a title, and by mastering this element, you set the stage for successful transactions.

CRAFTING KEYWORD-RICH TITLES

Creating keyword-rich titles is essential for optimizing your eBay listings for both visibility and relevance. Keywords are the terms and phrases that buyers use to search for items, making them crucial for your titles. This section covers how to identify these keywords and incorporate them effectively into your titles.

Tools and Techniques to Find the Best Keywords for Your Products

1. **eBay Search Bar Autocomplete:**
    - **How It Works:** Start typing a keyword related to your product in the eBay search bar and note the autocomplete suggestions. These suggestions are popular search terms used by buyers.
    - **Example:** If you're selling yoga mats, typing "yoga" may show autocomplete suggestions like "yoga mat non slip" or "yoga mat thick."
2. **Terapeak Product Research:**
    - **How It Works:** Available within eBay's Seller Hub under the "Research" tab, Terapeak provides insights into what buyers are searching for, how items are performing, and which terms are trending in your category.
    - **Benefit:** Terapeak offers data directly from eBay, making it extremely relevant and specific to what works on the platform.

3. **Google Keyword Planner:**
     - **How It Works:** Though Google's search engine differs from eBay, Keyword Planner can provide a broader perspective on what keywords people use when they start their product search online.
     - **Application:** Use it to find additional keywords that may not be as obvious within the eBay ecosystem.
4. **Competitor Analysis:**
     - **How It Works:** Look at listings from top sellers in your category. Note the common terms these successful listings use.
     - **Why It's Important:** If these keywords work for top sellers, they are likely optimized for high search volume and relevance.

How to Integrate Keywords Seamlessly into Your Titles Without Stuffing

1. **Prioritize Relevance:**
     - **Strategy:** Only use keywords that are directly related to your product. Forcing irrelevant keywords can confuse potential buyers and hurt your listing's performance.
     - **Example:** For a "waterproof camping tent," relevant keywords could be "camping," "tent," "waterproof," "outdoor," and "durable."
2. **Natural Language Integration:**
     - **Technique:** Incorporate keywords as part of a coherent and readable sentence, rather than a list of terms.
     - **Example:** Change "Tent Camping Outdoor Waterproof Durable" to "Waterproof Camping Tent - Durable Outdoor Shelter."

3. **Utilize Key Attributes:**
    - **How It Works:** Focus on keywords that highlight key attributes like condition, color, size, or uniqueness.
    - **Example:** "Red Yoga Mat 10mm Thick Non-Slip."
4. **Keyword Positioning:**
    - **Insight:** Place the most important keywords at the beginning of the title, as early visibility can impact click-through rates.
    - **Example:** "Vintage Rolex Watch - Rare 1950s Oyster Perpetual."
5. **Avoid Over-Optimization:**
    - **Advice:** While keywords are important, overusing them can make your title unreadable or appear spammy, which can deter buyers.
    - **Balance:** Ensure that the title sounds natural to human readers while containing necessary keywords for search algorithms.

By using these tools and techniques, you can craft titles that are not only rich in relevant keywords but also appealing to potential buyers. Remember, the goal of your title is not just to attract views but to attract the right views from interested buyers likely to make a purchase.

EXAMPLES OF WINNING EBAY TITLES

A successful eBay title is one that not only captures attention but also provides clear and concise information that meets the search intent of potential buyers. This section will break down the elements of effective titles and provide real-world examples to illustrate these points. Additionally, practice exercises will help you refine your headline-writing skills.

Breakdown of Successful eBay Titles

Example 1: "Apple MacBook Pro 13-inch 2020 M1 Chip 256GB SSD 8GB RAM Silver - Sealed"

- **Keywords Integrated:** Apple, MacBook Pro, 13-inch, 2020, M1 Chip, 256GB SSD, 8GB RAM, Silver.
- **Clarity and Specificity:** The title specifies the brand, model, size, year, processor, storage capacity, memory, color, and condition.
- **Searchable Terms:** This title is packed with terms potential buyers are likely to use when looking for this type of product, such as "M1 Chip," "256GB SSD," and "2020."

Example 2: "Nike Air Max 270 React Men's Running Shoes Sneakers Size 11 Black/White New"

- **Keywords Integrated:** Nike, Air Max 270, React, Men's, Running Shoes, Sneakers, Size 11, Black/White, New.
- **Informative:** It immediately tells the buyer everything they need to know about the product—brand, model,

type, size, color, and condition.
- **Targeted:** The title is tailored to attract buyers specifically looking for men's running shoes, making it highly effective.

Practice Exercises to Refine Your Headline-Writing Skills

Exercise 1: Write a Title for an Electronics Item
- **Product:** Samsung Galaxy S20 Ultra
- **Specifications:** 128GB, Cosmic Gray, Unlocked, 5G Capable
- **Condition:** Brand New

Task: Using the principles outlined, craft a title that includes all the necessary details.

Exercise 2: Write a Title for a Fashion Item
- **Product:** Gucci Marmont Matelassé Leather Mini Bag
- **Color:** Black
- **Condition:** Lightly Used

Task: Create a title that emphasizes the brand, model, material, size, color, and condition.

Exercise 3: Write a Title for a Collectible Item
- **Product:** 1950s Coca-Cola Vintage Wall Clock
- **Feature:** Glass Face, Battery Operated
- **Condition:** Good, working condition

Task: Develop a title that highlights the age, brand, uniqueness, and condition of the item.

Guidelines for Exercises:
1. **Start with the Brand and Model:** Always lead with the most searched terms, which are often the brand and specific model or type of product.
2. **Include Key Specifications:** For electronics, include specs like storage or special features; for fashion, focus on material or special characteristics; for collectibles,

denote any unique features or historical relevance.

3. **Specify Condition:** Always mention the condition to avoid ambiguity and attract the right buyers.
4. **Check Length:** Ensure your title does not exceed eBay's character limit, ensuring all critical information is visible.

These exercises are designed to help you practice the balance between including necessary information and keeping the title concise and to the point. As you refine your titles, remember that a successful eBay listing title is one that clearly communicates what is being sold, making it easy for buyers to find and understand the value of the item at a glance.

CHAPTER 2: DESCRIPTION POWERHOUSE

The Elements of a Powerful Description

A well-crafted product description is crucial for converting interested shoppers into buyers on eBay. The description not only provides essential information about the item but also serves as a platform to persuade and reassure potential buyers about the quality and value of the product. This section will explore the key components every eBay listing description must include and how to use formatting tools to enhance readability and engagement.

Key Components of Every Listing Description

1. Detailed Item Information:

- **Specifications:** Clearly list the product's specifications, such as size, weight, color, model, age, and technical features.
- **Condition:** Describe the condition of the item in detail, including any wear and tear, functionality issues, or if it's brand new.
- **Authenticity:** For branded items, emphasize authenticity to assure buyers they are getting a genuine product.

2. Unique Selling Points (USPs):

- Highlight what makes your product stand out. This

could be anything from a limited edition feature, a hard-to-find color, or an included accessory that is not commonly offered.

3. Usage Instructions or Suggestions:
- Suggest how the product can be used or potential benefits. For example, if you're selling a camera, mention how it's perfect for both professional photography and casual use.

4. Warranty and Return Information:
- Provide details about warranty coverage or your return policy to reassure buyers about the after-purchase support.

5. Shipping Details:
- Outline your shipping process, options, costs, and any shipping promotions like free shipping. Mention how items will be packed and the expected delivery times.

Using Formatting Tools to Enhance Readability and Engagement

Effective Use of HTML Formatting:
- **Bold and Italics:** Use bold for headings and italics to emphasize key points or unique features. For example, use bold for section headers like "Specifications," "Condition," and "Shipping Details."
- **Bullet Points:** Use bullet points to break down information into easily digestible parts. This is particularly useful for specifications and features.
- **Paragraph Breaks:** Keep paragraphs short – ideally 2-3 sentences each. This makes the description easier to scan and read.
- **Font Sizes:** Use varying font sizes to create a hierarchy of information. Larger fonts for headings and smaller fonts for detailed information help guide the reader's eye through the description.

Including High-Quality Images and Videos:
- Embed high-quality images or videos within the description to show the product from multiple angles or in use. Ensure these visuals are optimized for quick loading.

Using Color Wisely:
- Use color sparingly to draw attention to calls to action or special offers. Ensure the color contrasts well with the background for readability.

Creating a Responsive Design:
- Ensure that the description looks good on both desktops and mobile devices. Most eBay buyers use mobile devices, so a mobile-friendly presentation is essential.

Example of a Well-Formatted Description:

Product Overview:
- **Brand:** Nikon
- **Model:** D3500 DSLR Camera
- **Condition:** Brand new, sealed in box

Key Features:
- **Resolution:** 24.2 megapixels for stunning clarity
- **Lens:** Comes with an 18-55mm VR lens kit
- **Connectivity:** Built-in Bluetooth for easy sharing

Why Choose the Nikon D3500?
- Ideal for entry-level photographers and hobbyists
- Lightweight and compact design
- User-friendly interface

Shipping Information:
- Ships within 24 hours via FedEx Ground
- Free shipping on orders over $50
- Securely packaged to ensure safe delivery

Warranty:

- 1-year manufacturer warranty included
- 30-day money-back guarantee if not satisfied

Using these formatting tools and structuring your content thoughtfully can significantly improve the clarity and appeal of your eBay listings, thus helping to increase sales and customer satisfaction.

Incorporating Keywords Naturally
- Strategies for weaving keywords into your descriptions for better SEO without sacrificing readability.
- Monitoring and adjusting your keyword strategy based on performance metrics.

Writing Descriptions that Sell
- Tips for highlighting key features and benefits that resonate with buyers.
- Techniques for addressing potential buyer concerns preemptively.

CHAPTER 3: COMPELLING CONTENT

Showcasing Your Product's Value Proposition

Effectively communicating the value proposition of your product is crucial in distinguishing it from competitors and appealing to potential buyers on a deeper level. This involves highlighting the unique selling points (USPs) and using storytelling techniques to forge an emotional connection with your audience. This section will guide you through the steps to achieve this in your eBay listings.

Identifying and Communicating Unique Selling Points

1. Define What Makes Your Product Unique:

- **Functionality:** Does your product offer a feature or function that others don't? For example, a smartphone with an exceptionally long battery life.
- **Quality:** Is your product made from higher quality materials or through superior craftsmanship? Mention specifics like "handcrafted leather" or "surgical-grade stainless steel."
- **Exclusivity:** Is your item rare, limited edition, or available for a limited time? Highlight exclusivity that can drive the decision to purchase sooner rather than later.
- **Price:** Do you offer the best value for the price compared

to similar items? If your pricing is competitive, make sure to point it out.

2. Articulate the Benefits:
- Rather than just listing features, explain how these features benefit the user. Turn "water-resistant up to 30 meters" into "enjoy swimming or snorkeling without worry with our water-resistant watch."

3. Solve a Problem:
- Identify common problems faced by your target customers and explain how your product solves them. If you're selling a multi-port USB charger, mention how it solves the problem of too many devices and not enough outlets.

Using Storytelling to Connect Emotionally

1. Create Relatable Scenarios:
- Craft scenarios or stories where potential buyers can imagine using your product. For a camera, paint a picture of capturing beautiful family memories at a reunion or an adventurous trip.

2. Use Reviews and Testimonials:
- Incorporate customer testimonials that tell a story of how the product improved their life or solved a specific problem. This not only serves as social proof but also lets potential buyers see real-life applications.

3. Connect to Larger Themes:
- Link your product to broader emotional themes such as freedom, security, or happiness. For instance, if you're selling a bike lock, connect it to the peace of mind it brings, allowing cyclists to feel secure when they need to leave their bike unattended.

4. Be Authentic:
- Authenticity resonates deeply with consumers. Share a true story about the origins of your product or why it

was created. If you're selling handmade jewelry, share your artistic journey or the inspiration behind your designs.

Example of an eBay Description Using Storytelling

Unlock the Joy of Photography with the Canon EOS Rebel T7 DSLR Camera

Imagine capturing the stunning colors of a sunset or the joyful smile of your child blowing out birthday candles. The Canon EOS Rebel T7 makes this possible with its user-friendly features and professional-quality images. Whether you're a beginner or a seasoned pro, this camera is designed to bring your creative vision to life.

Why Choose the Canon EOS Rebel T7?

- **Capture Every Detail:** 24.1 Megapixel sensor ensures high-resolution images that make your photos look professional.
- **Easy Sharing:** Built-in Wi-Fi and NFC technology let you share your favorite moments with friends and family in seconds.
- **All-Day Shooting Comfort:** Designed with a lightweight frame and intuitive controls to offer comfort and ease during extended shooting sessions.

Don't just take our word for it. Here's what John D., a satisfied customer, had to say: "I took the Rebel T7 on my trip to the Grand Canyon, and the photos were breathtaking. It was easy to carry around, and the battery lasted all day. Highly recommend for anyone who loves traveling and photography!"

Special Offer:

- *Order today and get a free camera bag to start your photography journey in style. Capture the moments that matter with Canon EOS Rebel T7.*

By focusing on the unique selling points through a blend of factual and emotional content, you can significantly enhance the attractiveness of your eBay listings. This approach not only informs but also engages potential buyers, increasing the likelihood of converting interest into sales.

ENHANCING PERCEIVED VALUE THROUGH SCARCITY AND URGENCY

Incorporating the principles of scarcity and urgency into your eBay listings can dramatically increase interest and compel buyers to act quickly. However, it's crucial to implement these tactics in a way that feels natural and not overly aggressive. This section explores how to effectively use scarcity and urgency to enhance perceived value and accelerate decision-making processes among potential buyers.

Applying Scarcity

1. Limited Quantity:

- **How to Use:** Clearly state when only a few items are left in stock. For example, adding a note such as "Only 3 left in stock" naturally increases the item's perceived rarity and value.
- **Example:** "Hurry! Only 3 units remaining at this price!"

2. Special Editions:

- **How to Use:** Highlight if the product is a limited edition or available for a limited time. This not only makes the item seem exclusive but also more desirable.
- **Example:** "Limited Edition Designer Handbag - Only 20 made worldwide!"

3. Unique Features:

- **How to Use:** If your product has unique features not found in other similar items, make sure to emphasize these aspects.
- **Example:** "Exclusive features available only in this model—get yours before they're gone!"

Implementing Urgency

1. Time-Limited Offers:

- **How to Use:** Introduce offers that are available for a limited time. This encourages buyers to make a purchase decision sooner rather than later.
- **Example:** "Sale ends in 24 hours! Act now to save 20%!"

2. Countdown Timers:

- **How to Use:** Incorporating a countdown timer for deals or the end of an auction can visually enhance the urgency.
- **Example:** Display a countdown timer on the listing page, showing time ticking down until the offer expires.

3. Last Chance Messages:

- **How to Use:** Communicate urgency through messages that indicate an opportunity is about to expire.
- **Example:** "Last chance to buy at this price!" or "Final day to order with guaranteed delivery before Christmas!"

Examples of Effective Use in eBay Listings

Example 1:

- **Product:** Men's Limited-Edition Watches
- **Listing Title:** "Grab it Before Time Runs Out: Men's Chronograph Watch - Only 10 Left!"
- **Description:** "Experience exclusivity with our limited-edition chronograph watch. With only 10 pieces available worldwide, secure yours before they disappear forever. Don't miss this unique opportunity to own a

rare piece of craftsmanship. Offer ends soon!"

Example 2:
- **Product:** High-End DSLR Camera Bundle
- **Listing Title:** "48-Hour Flash Sale: Professional DSLR Camera Kit - Save 15%!"
- **Description:** "Elevate your photography with our professional DSLR camera kit, now at 15% off for the next 48 hours. Capture stunning photos with state-of-the-art technology. Time is running out to claim this deal—shop now to avoid disappointment!"

Using Scarcity and Urgency Wisely:
- When applying these principles, ensure the claims are genuine. Misleading customers can lead to dissatisfaction and damage your reputation. Always be transparent about stock levels or the availability of special offers.

By thoughtfully integrating scarcity and urgency into your eBay listings, you create compelling reasons for buyers to act quickly, thus enhancing the perceived value of your items and increasing your sales velocity.

CHAPTER 4: CALL TO ACTION PROWESS

What Makes an Effective Call to Action

A call to action (CTA) is a crucial component of any eBay listing, serving as the bridge between browsing and buying. Understanding the psychology behind a compelling CTA and following some best practices can significantly enhance the effectiveness of your sales efforts. This section explores the key elements that make a CTA persuasive and provides guidelines on what to do and what to avoid.

The Psychology Behind Persuasive Calls to Action

1. Clarity and Simplicity:

- **Psychological Principle:** Decision fatigue. Consumers can become overwhelmed when presented with too many choices or complicated instructions. A clear and simple CTA reduces mental strain and makes the decision process easier.
- **Application:** Use direct language that leaves no room for ambiguity about what the buyer should do next, such as "Buy Now," "Add to Cart," or "Place Your Bid."

2. Urgency and Scarcity:

- **Psychological Principle:** Fear of missing out (FOMO). Buyers are more likely to take action if they perceive that an opportunity is limited.
- **Application:** Incorporate elements of urgency and scarcity in your CTAs, like "Limited Offer," "Only a Few

Left," or "Offer Ends Soon."

3. Value Proposition:
- **Psychological Principle:** Reward system. Customers are more inclined to take action if they feel they are getting a tangible benefit or solving a problem.
- **Application:** Highlight the benefit clearly in the CTA, such as "Save 20% Today" or "Get Free Shipping."

The Dos and Don'ts of Creating Effective CTAs

Do:
- **Be Specific:** Tell your buyers exactly what you want them to do. Use action-oriented verbs that provoke enthusiasm and excitement.
- **Create a Sense of Urgency:** Without being pushy, make it clear that acting now is in their best interest.
- **Use Contrasting Colors:** Make your CTA button or link stand out with colors that contrast well with the rest of your listing but still fit within your overall design scheme.
- **Keep It Visible:** Place your CTA in an easy-to-find location that naturally flows from the rest of the content. Ideally, it should be visible without the need for scrolling.
- **Test and Refine:** Use A/B testing for different CTAs to see which performs better. Adjust based on customer feedback and analytics.

Don't:
- **Overwhelm with Options:** Avoid giving too many options or using multiple CTAs that lead to different actions. Focus on one primary CTA per listing.
- **Use Generic Language:** "Click here" doesn't tell your buyer anything about why they should take that action. Always link the action to a specific benefit or outcome.
- **Hide Your CTA:** If buyers can't find your CTA easily,

they won't convert. Avoid placing CTAs in places that are typically ignored, like the very bottom of the listing or surrounded by clutter.

- **Forget Mobile Users:** Ensure your CTA is easily clickable on mobile devices. Buttons should be large enough to tap and spaced well from other links to avoid errors.
- **Ignore Design:** A CTA that looks out of place or visually unappealing can deter users. Make sure your CTA is well-integrated into the overall design of your listing.

Example of an Effective CTA in an eBay Listing

Product: Gourmet Coffee Beans, 1 lb Bag

- **CTA:** "Order Now to Enjoy Fresh, Artisan Coffee with Free Expedited Shipping!"
- **Why It Works:** This CTA is clear, provides a direct benefit (freshness and free shipping), and uses urgent language that encourages immediate action.

By crafting CTAs that are clear, compelling, and aligned with the buyers' interests, you can significantly increase the chances of converting interest into actual sales on eBay. Remember, the effectiveness of your CTA can directly impact your bottom line, so it's worth spending the time to get it right.

CRAFTING CLEAR AND CONCISE CALLS TO ACTION

A strong call to action (CTA) is not just a button on your eBay listing—it's the key phrase that compels a buyer to take the next step, whether that's making a purchase, watching a product video, or signing up for a newsletter. Effective CTAs lead to higher conversion rates and better sales performance. Below is a step-by-step guide to writing CTAs that lead to clicks, followed by tips on analyzing and optimizing these crucial elements.

Step-by-Step Guide to Writing Effective CTAs

Step 1: Start with a Strong Command Verb

- Begin your CTA with a verb that prompts action, such as "Buy," "Shop," "Order," "Discover," or "Start." Choose a verb that reflects the level of engagement you want from the buyer.

Step 2: Use Words that Provoke Emotion or Enthusiasm

- The right words can evoke a sense of excitement and urgency. Words like "Now," "Today," "Exclusive," or "Limited" can add a sense of urgency; "Save," "Discover," "Build," or "Join" can generate enthusiasm.

Step 3: Give a Reason Why

- Explain why they should take the action. What's in it for them? This could be a discount, free shipping, or access to exclusive products. For example, "Buy Now and Save

20%," or "Order Today for Free Shipping!"

Step 4: Fear of Missing Out (FOMO)
- Incorporate elements of scarcity and urgency. If applicable, make it clear that they need to act quickly to benefit from the offer.

Step 5: Visual Design
- Ensure your CTA button or link is visually striking. Use colors that stand out from the rest of the page but still fit within the overall design. The button should be easy to find and large enough to click on, especially for mobile users.

Step 6: Placement
- Place your CTA where it's easy to see and follows logically from the flow of the page content. Ideally, viewers should not have to scroll excessively to find it.

Step 7: Keep It Short
- The best CTAs are brief and to the point. Limit your CTA to no more than five to seven words to ensure it's easily digestible at a glance.

Analyzing and Optimizing Your CTAs

1. Track Click-through Rates (CTR)
- The CTR will tell you what percentage of visitors are actually clicking on your CTA. A low CTR might indicate that your CTA is not compelling enough or is poorly placed.

2. Use A/B Testing
- Test different versions of your CTAs to see which performs better. Change one variable at a time, such as the color, wording, or placement, and compare the results. This can help you fine-tune what works best for your audience.

3. Analyze Conversion Rates

- It's not just about clicks; it's about what those clicks lead to. Monitor how many clicks on your CTA actually result in sales or other desired outcomes. This metric will help you measure the effectiveness of your CTA in achieving your business objectives.

4. Gather User Feedback

- Sometimes, direct feedback from users can provide insights that data alone cannot. Ask customers through follow-up emails or during customer service interactions how they felt about the purchasing process and whether the CTA was clear.

5. Monitor and Adapt

- Regularly review the performance of your CTAs and make adjustments as needed. Consumer behavior and market trends change, so what works today might not work tomorrow.

Example of an Optimized CTA in an eBay Listing

Before: "Click here to buy"

- **After A/B Testing:** "Buy Now - Save 15% Today Only!"
- **Improvements Made:** Added urgency ("Today Only"), a direct action verb ("Buy"), and a clear benefit ("Save 15%").

By crafting CTAs that are not only clear and concise but also strategically designed and placed, you can significantly increase the likelihood of turning visitors into buyers. Remember, a great CTA is an essential tool for closing sales and enhancing the user experience on your eBay listings.

CHAPTER 5: VISUAL STRATEGIES THAT SELL

Using High-Quality Images to Enhance Listings

High-quality images are essential for successful eBay listings. They not only attract attention but also significantly influence a buyer's decision-making process by providing a visual confirmation of the item's description. Here's how you can take professional-grade photos with common devices and edit them to make your listings stand out.

Tips for Taking Professional-Grade Photos with Common Devices

1. Use the Right Equipment:
- **Smartphone:** Modern smartphones are equipped with cameras that can take exceptionally high-quality photos. Use the highest resolution setting available.
- **Camera:** If available, use a DSLR or a mirrorless camera for even higher quality images.

2. Lighting is Key:
- **Natural Light:** Whenever possible, use natural light. Take photos during the day near windows or in a well-lit area outside. Avoid direct sunlight as it can cause harsh shadows.
- **Artificial Light:** If natural light isn't available, use soft box lights or ring lights to create a well-lit setting

without harsh shadows.

3. Stable Setup:
- Use a tripod or stable surface to avoid blurry images. Even slight hand movements can reduce the sharpness of a photo.

4. Clear Background:
- Use a neutral, uncluttered background to ensure the focus remains on the item. Plain backgrounds, like white or light gray, are typically best as they don't distract from the product.

5. Multiple Angles:
- Take multiple shots from various angles to fully showcase the item. Include top, front, side views, and any unique details or features.

6. Focus on Details:
- Use the macro mode for close-up shots to capture details or any imperfections, which can be crucial for buyer confidence and reducing returns.

Editing and Formatting Your Images to Stand Out

1. Basic Editing:
- **Crop:** Trim photos to ensure the product fills the frame appropriately, which enhances the item's visibility in thumbnail views.
- **Adjust Brightness and Contrast:** Improve image quality by adjusting the brightness and contrast to make the photos appear more vibrant and clear.
- **Sharpen:** Slightly sharpen images to enhance detail, especially if the original image is slightly soft.

2. Maintain Consistency:
- Ensure all your images maintain a consistent look in terms of lighting, background, and editing style. Consistency gives your listings a professional

appearance.

3. Optimize for Load Times:
- Resize images to balance quality and load time. Large images can slow down page loading, which might deter potential buyers. Aim for a resolution that is high enough for clarity but not so high that it impacts website performance.

4. Use Multiple Images:
- eBay allows up to 12 images for free. Use this to your advantage by uploading multiple photos to provide a comprehensive view of the item.

5. Highlight Key Features:
- Use image editing tools to add text overlays or pointers to highlight key features or imperfections. However, keep such edits minimal to avoid cluttering the image.

6. Testing:
- View your images on different devices to ensure they look good on desktop monitors as well as mobile devices. Often, buyers use mobile devices, so your images must be optimized for smaller screens as well.

Example of Effective Image Use in an eBay Listing

Consider a listing for a vintage wristwatch:
- **Main Image:** Front view of the watch, taken in soft natural light with a plain white background.
- **Additional Images:** Close-ups of the watch face, back, and any engravings or details, side profile, and one with the watch being worn (to show scale).
- **Editing:** Slight brightness and contrast adjustments to ensure the watch's color and details are vivid and clear.

By following these guidelines, you can create visually appealing and effective listings on eBay that not only draw in buyers with their professionalism but also provide all the visual information needed to secure a purchase. High-quality images can significantly enhance the perceived value of your items and lead to higher satisfaction and fewer returns from buyers.

INCORPORATING VIDEOS AND OTHER MEDIA

Adding video to your eBay listings can significantly enhance the buyer's shopping experience by providing a dynamic and interactive view of your products. Videos can help to convey more information than photos alone, offer a closer look at the item's condition and features, and build a higher level of trust with potential buyers. This section will explore the benefits of integrating video into your listings and offer simple tools and techniques for creating compelling video content.

Benefits of Adding Video to Your Listings

1. Enhanced Engagement:

- **Visual Appeal:** Videos capture attention more effectively than static images, keeping potential buyers on your listing longer.
- **Interactive Experience:** Videos allow buyers to see the product in action, which can be particularly beneficial for items like electronics, mechanical devices, or fashion pieces.

2. Improved Transparency:

- **Detail Showcase:** A video can highlight aspects of the product that are hard to convey through photos alone, such as the functionality of a device or the flow of a fabric.

- **Condition Verification:** Videos provide a 360-degree view, helping to reassure buyers about the quality and condition of the item, reducing the likelihood of returns due to unmet expectations.

3. **Increased Conversion Rates:**
   - **Confidence Building:** By providing a thorough look at the product, videos can help reduce buyer hesitation and encourage quicker purchasing decisions.
   - **Emotional Connection:** Videos can create a stronger emotional connection by showing the product in a real-life context, which can influence buying behavior positively.

Tools and Techniques for Creating Compelling Video Content

1. Tools for Video Creation:
- **Smartphones:** Most modern smartphones have sufficient video quality for creating listing videos. Use a smartphone with a good camera, ideally one that can shoot in at least 1080p.
- **Cameras:** For higher-quality videos, consider using a DSLR or mirrorless camera.
- **Stabilizing Equipment:** Use tripods or gimbals to ensure your video is steady and professional-looking.

2. Lighting and Sound:
- **Lighting:** Good lighting is crucial for video quality. Use natural light where possible or invest in softbox lights or ring lights.
- **Sound:** If your video includes speaking, use a good-quality microphone to ensure clear audio. Consider lapel mics or external microphones that can attach to your phone or camera.

3. Video Editing Software:
- **Beginner-Friendly Options:** Use simple editing tools like iMovie (for Mac users), Windows Movie Maker, or

smartphone apps like InShot or Adobe Premiere Rush.
- **Advanced Tools:** For more sophisticated editing, software like Adobe Premiere Pro or Final Cut Pro offers extensive features and effects.

4. Content Structure:

- **Introduction:** Start with a brief introduction of what the video will cover.
- **Demonstration:** Show the product in use. For example, demonstrate how a gadget works, showcase the different features of a backpack, or model a piece of clothing.
- **Details:** Zoom in on important features, details, and any condition issues to be transparent.
- **Call to Action:** End with a call to action, encouraging viewers to make a purchase or check out other listings.

5. Optimizing Video Length:

- Keep your videos concise. A good rule of thumb is to aim for 30 seconds to 2 minutes, long enough to provide valuable content but short enough to maintain the viewer's attention.

Example of Effective Video Usage

For a vintage camera listing:

- **Introduction:** Briefly introduce the camera model and its significance.
- **Visual Tour:** Provide a hands-on tour of the camera, highlighting its vintage condition and unique features.
- **Function Demonstration:** Show the camera in action, perhaps even including sample photos taken with the camera.
- **Conclusion:** Recap the features and invite viewers to bid or purchase.

By incorporating videos into your eBay listings, you can significantly enhance how your products are presented, making them more attractive to potential buyers. Videos help to bridge the gap between online shopping and the tangible in-store experience, providing buyers with a clearer, more confident path to purchase.

CHAPTER 6: BUILDING TRUST AND CREDIBILITY

Detailed Descriptions and Transparent Policies

Creating trust with potential buyers on eBay involves providing comprehensive product descriptions and clear, fair policies. This trust is crucial not only for securing a sale but also for building a reputation as a reliable seller, which can encourage repeat business. Here's how to craft detailed descriptions and set transparent policies effectively.

Establishing Trust Through Comprehensive Product Descriptions

1. Complete and Accurate Information:
- **Essentials:** Always include the basics—size, color, material, model, age, and condition of the item.
- **Specifics:** Go beyond the basics to include specific features or any unique aspects that might interest a buyer, such as the origin of a handmade product or any technological innovations in an electronic device.

2. Honesty About Condition:
- **Transparency:** Be upfront about any defects, wear, or functionality issues. This honesty prevents disputes and negative feedback from buyers who feel misled.
- **Visual Proof:** Accompany descriptions of any flaws or

damage with photographs. This visual evidence helps to validate your textual description and adds to your credibility.

3. Contextual Information:
- **Usage Tips:** Provide suggestions on how the item can be used, which can be particularly helpful for items with multiple functions or complex features.
- **Background Story:** If applicable, include the backstory of the item, especially for antiques, collectibles, or artisan items. This adds emotional value and can make the item more appealing.

4. Keyword Optimization:
- **Search Visibility:** Use relevant keywords naturally within your descriptions. This improves search visibility on eBay and search engines, making it easier for buyers to find your listing.

Setting Clear and Fair Return Policies

1. Return Policy Basics:
- **Time Frame:** Specify the time frame in which a return is accepted (e.g., 30 days after purchase).
- **Condition of Returns:** Clearly state the condition in which items must be returned (e.g., unworn, with tags, original packaging).
- **Restocking Fees:** If you apply restocking fees, disclose this upfront to avoid surprises and potential buyer dissatisfaction.

2. Transparent Process:
- **Step-by-Step Instructions:** Provide clear instructions for how returns are handled, including where to send the item, how the refund is issued, and who pays for return shipping (seller or buyer).
- **Speed of Refund:** State how quickly the refund will be processed once the item is received.

3. **Warranty Information:**
   - **Coverage Details:** If your products come with a warranty, detail what the warranty covers, the duration of the warranty, and how buyers can claim it.
   - **Contact Information:** Provide a direct way for buyers to contact you with warranty issues.

4. **Exceptions and Special Cases:**
   - **Clarifications:** If certain items are non-returnable (such as final sale items or personalized goods), make this explicitly clear in the listing.
   - **Flexibility:** Consider offering flexibility for exceptional circumstances, such as extending the return period during holidays.

Example of a Well-Crafted eBay Listing Description

Product: Handcrafted Mahogany Wooden Bowl

Description: Experience the warmth and beauty of a handcrafted mahogany bowl. Each bowl is unique, featuring rich, deep patterns that only natural wood can offer. Perfect for a rustic yet elegant home decor piece, or as a special gift.

Specifications:
- **Material:** 100% Solid Mahogany Wood
- **Diameter:** 12 inches
- **Height:** 6 inches
- **Finish:** Natural oil for a durable and smooth surface
- **Condition:** Brand new, crafted by local artisans

Features:
- **Versatile Use:** Ideal for serving salads or as a decorative centerpiece.
- **Eco-Friendly:** Sourced from sustainable forests.

Care Instructions: Hand wash with mild soap and dry immediately. Not dishwasher safe.

Return Policy:
- **30-Day Returns:** Accepted if the item is returned in its original condition and packaging.
- **Process:** Contact us through eBay messages for a return label.
- **Refund:** Issued within 2 business days of receiving the returned item.

By providing detailed descriptions and transparent policies, you not only enhance buyer trust but also minimize the risk of returns and disputes. This thoroughness in your eBay listings will contribute significantly to a positive selling experience and help foster lasting customer relationships.

CHAPTER 7: COMPETITIVE PRICING STRATEGIES

Setting the Right Price

Effective pricing is crucial for success on eBay, as it directly influences both your sales volume and profit margins. Understanding how to conduct competitive pricing analysis and choosing the right pricing strategy—whether it's setting an auction or a "Buy It Now" price—can make a significant difference. This section will guide you through these critical aspects to help you set optimal prices for your listings.

Tools and Techniques for Competitive Pricing Analysis

1. Use eBay's Completed Listings:
- **How It Works:** Search for completed sales of items similar to yours on eBay to see what prices they achieved. This feature is accessible under the "Advanced Search" options.
- **Benefits:** Understanding what buyers are willing to pay for similar items can help you set a realistic and competitive price.

2. Utilize Terapeak:
- **Tool Description:** eBay provides a tool called Terapeak, available in the Seller Hub, which offers insights into pricing trends, demand, and competition for products similar to yours.

- **Application:** Use Terapeak to analyze market data over specific periods to inform your pricing strategy based on historical and current market conditions.

3. Monitor Your Competitors:
- **Regular Checks:** Keep an eye on how your direct competitors are pricing similar items. Consider setting up alerts for specific keywords related to your products.
- **Adjust Accordingly:** If you notice a trend or a change in the pricing strategies of your competitors, consider whether you need to adjust your prices to stay competitive.

4. Consider Your Costs:
- **Total Costs:** Make sure your pricing covers all your costs, including sourcing, eBay fees, shipping, and any other overheads. This ensures your pricing strategy is sustainable.

Deciding Between Auction and "Buy It Now"

1. When to Use Auction:
- **Ideal for Rare or Collectible Items:** Auctions can be the best choice for items that are rare, collectible, or where the market value isn't clearly defined. Bidding wars can drive up the price.
- **Uncertain Demand:** If you're unsure about the demand for an item, an auction can help establish its market value.
- **Quick Sales:** Auctions can be set to last for 1, 3, 5, 7, or 10 days, providing a faster turnaround time if needed.

2. When to Use "Buy It Now":
- **High-Demand Items:** For items that have a steady, predictable demand, "Buy It Now" ensures that you get the price you want without the uncertainty of an auction.
- **Convenience for Buyers:** Some buyers prefer the

convenience of purchasing immediately rather than waiting for an auction to end.
- **Price Control:** This method gives you complete control over the pricing, which is useful for items with a known market value or when you have a clear price point that needs to be met.

3. Combining Both Methods:
- **Strategy:** eBay allows sellers to list an item with both an auction and a "Buy It Now" option. Once a bid is placed that meets or exceeds the minimum bid threshold, the "Buy It Now" option usually disappears.
- **Benefits:** This approach allows you to attract both types of buyers: those looking for the potential deal through an auction and those who prefer to purchase immediately.

Example of Pricing Strategy Application

Product: Vintage Designer Sunglasses
- **Auction:** Start the bidding at a lower price, such as $50, to attract bidders looking for a deal.
- **Buy It Now:** Set the "Buy It Now" price based on market research at $150, a fair market value that reflects the item's worth and desirability.

By effectively utilizing tools for competitive analysis and choosing the appropriate pricing strategy, you can optimize your sales potential on eBay. Each method has its benefits, and your choice should align with the specific circumstances of the item you are selling and your overall business goals.

Adjusting Prices Based on Market Response

MONITORING SALES DATA TO UNDERSTAND PRICING EFFECTIVENESS

Keeping a close eye on sales data is critical for any eBay seller looking to understand the effectiveness of their pricing strategy. By analyzing this data, you can make informed decisions about when and how to adjust prices to maximize sales and revenue. Here's how to effectively monitor and adjust your pricing on eBay.

Monitoring Sales Data

1. Use eBay's Seller Hub Reports:
- **Sales Reports:** eBay's Seller Hub offers detailed reports that track your sales performance over time. These reports provide insights into how different pricing strategies impact sales.
- **Traffic Reports:** Understand where your buyers come from and what devices they use. This data can help you identify buying patterns and optimize your listings for those platforms.

2. Track Competitor Pricing:
- **Competitive Analysis:** Regularly check the prices of similar listings. Note any trends or changes in how competitors price items similar to yours.
- **Automated Tools:** Consider using tools like

RepricerExpress or StreetPricer, which automate the tracking of competitor prices and provide alerts when changes occur.

3. Analyze Seasonal and Market Trends:
- **Seasonality:** Some products may see a spike in demand during certain times of the year. Adjusting prices ahead of these trends can help you capitalize on increased demand.
- **Market Changes:** Keep an eye on broader market trends that might affect pricing strategies, such as new product releases or changes in consumer spending habits.

Adjusting Prices Dynamically

1. Set Automated Pricing Rules:
- **eBay Automated Rules:** eBay allows sellers to set up rules that automatically adjust prices based on certain criteria, such as undercutting the lowest competitor price by a small percentage.
- **Consider Margins:** Ensure that any automated rules take into account your profit margins. It's important to stay competitive without sacrificing profitability.

2. Implement Promotional Pricing:
- **Sales and Discounts:** Use eBay's promotional tools to offer temporary discounts on your products. This can be particularly effective during slow sales periods or when you have excess inventory.
- **Markdown Manager:** eBay's Markdown Manager tool can help you manage and schedule sales, allowing you to attract more buyers with time-limited offers.

3. Test and Learn:
- **A/B Testing:** Experiment with different prices for the same product to see which generates more sales. This can be an effective way to find the optimal price point.
- **Feedback Loop:** Use customer feedback and sales data

to continuously refine your pricing strategy. If buyers frequently negotiate prices or make offers below your listed price, it may be a sign to adjust your pricing downwards.

4. Respond to Real-Time Data:

- **Quick Adjustments:** Be prepared to adjust prices quickly in response to external factors such as changes in supply costs, competitor pricing, or shifts in consumer demand.
- **Monitor Performance:** After making adjustments, monitor the performance closely to assess the impact. This can help you understand the effectiveness of your pricing strategy and make further refinements.

Example Scenario: Dynamic Pricing in Action

Product: High-end digital cameras

- **Initial Strategy:** Price your product competitively based on a survey of similar items.
- **Seasonal Adjustment:** Increase prices slightly during peak periods such as holidays when demand for electronics is high.
- **Promotional Discount:** Offer a 10% discount for a limited time during a slow sales month to stimulate interest.
- **Post-Promotion:** Evaluate sales data post-promotion to determine if the discount helped clear inventory without significantly impacting profit margins.

By actively monitoring and dynamically adjusting your pricing strategies based on comprehensive sales data and market trends, you can maximize both sales volume and profitability on eBay. This proactive approach allows you to stay competitive and responsive to changes in consumer behavior and market conditions.

CONCLUSION

Bringing It All Together

To succeed on eBay, it's crucial to deploy a range of strategies effectively. From crafting compelling titles and descriptions to choosing the right pricing and promotional tactics, every element plays a significant role in attracting and converting buyers. Here's a recap of the key strategies covered and a checklist to ensure your eBay listings are optimized for high conversion.

Recap of Key Strategies

1. Compelling Titles and Descriptions:
- Utilize keyword-rich, informative titles to improve visibility and attract buyers.
- Create detailed, honest descriptions that provide all necessary product information, highlight unique selling points, and address potential buyer concerns.

2. High-Quality Images and Videos:
- Incorporate professional-grade photos using good lighting and clear backgrounds.
- Add videos to showcase the product's features and usability, enhancing buyer trust and engagement.

3. Effective Pricing Strategies:
- Conduct competitive pricing analysis using tools like eBay's completed listings and Terapeak.
- Choose between auction and "Buy It Now" based on the product type and market demand.

4. Dynamic Pricing Adjustments:

- Set automated pricing rules to remain competitive without constant manual adjustments.
- Use promotional pricing strategically to boost sales during specific periods.

5. Clear and Fair Policies:
- Establish transparent return policies and detailed warranty information to build trust and reduce buyer hesitation.

6. Calls to Action:
- Craft clear and compelling calls to action that encourage immediate purchases, using urgency and clear benefits to motivate buyers.

Checklist for High-Converting eBay Listings

Title and Description:
- Title includes main keywords and is clear and concise.
- Description is detailed, highlighting key features and benefits.
- All item specifics are filled out to improve visibility in search results.

Images and Media:
- Multiple high-quality images from various angles.
- Video included if applicable, showing the product in use.
- Images and video are optimized for both desktop and mobile viewing.

Pricing and Promotion:
- Price is competitive based on market research.
- Consideration of "Auction" or "Buy It Now" based on item and strategy.
- Promotions and discounts are used strategically to increase sales velocity.

Policies and Transparency:

- Return policy is clearly stated and reasonable.
- Warranty or guarantee details (if applicable) are provided.
- Shipping costs and methods are clearly outlined.

Calls to Action:
- CTA is prominently placed and encourages immediate action.
- CTA text is compelling, utilizing urgency or exclusivity where appropriate.

Review and Optimization:
- Listings are regularly reviewed and updated based on performance data.
- Feedback from buyers is considered to continuously improve the listing quality.
- A/B testing conducted on different elements like prices, titles, and CTAs to find the most effective options.

By following these guidelines and regularly revisiting each component of your eBay listings, you can significantly enhance your ability to attract and convert more buyers. Success on eBay requires not just great products but also a strategic approach to presentation and sales tactics, ensuring that every listing is crafted to meet the needs and preferences of potential buyers.

Continual Improvement

STAYING UPDATED WITH EBAY'S CHANGING ALGORITHMS AND BUYER PREFERENCES

In the dynamic marketplace of eBay, staying informed about changes in algorithms and shifts in buyer preferences is crucial for maintaining and enhancing your sales performance. Regular updates to your strategy based on these changes can help you stay competitive and responsive to the market. Here are strategies to keep you updated and adaptive.

Keeping Up with eBay's Algorithm Changes

1. Regularly Visit eBay Seller Updates:

- **Action:** eBay frequently posts updates about changes to its platform, policies, and algorithms on its Seller Center. Make it a habit to check these updates to stay informed about new features and adjustments.

2. Participate in eBay Community and Forums:

- **Action:** Engage with other sellers in eBay's community forums. These can be a goldmine for insights on algorithm changes, as sellers often share their experiences and strategies for adapting to new updates.

3. Subscribe to eBay Newsletters:

- **Action:** eBay offers newsletters that can keep you updated on the latest news and tips. These are especially useful for learning about upcoming changes before they are implemented.

4. Attend eBay Seller Events:
- **Action:** eBay occasionally hosts events and webinars that can provide deeper insights into platform changes and new selling tools. Attending these events can also help you network with other sellers and eBay staff.

Understanding Buyer Preferences

1. Monitor Feedback and Reviews:
- **Action:** Regularly review feedback from your buyers. Pay attention to comments about what they like and dislike. This direct feedback can be invaluable in adjusting your listings to better meet buyer expectations.

2. Analyze Sales Data:
- **Action:** Use tools like eBay's Seller Hub to analyze which items are performing well and which aren't. Look for patterns in sales data that may indicate a shift in buyer preferences.

3. Stay Informed on Consumer Trends:
- **Action:** Keep abreast of broader market trends by reading industry news, following market research reports, and monitoring social media to understand what products are gaining popularity.

Continuously Testing and Refining Listing Strategies

1. Experiment with Listing Elements:
- **Action:** Regularly test different aspects of your listings, such as titles, descriptions, pricing strategies, and photos. Use A/B testing to compare performance and determine which elements resonate most with buyers.

2. Adjust Based on Season and Market Conditions:

- **Action:** Be prepared to adjust your listings based on seasonal changes and current market conditions. For example, emphasize different product features that may become more relevant during certain times of the year.

3. Use Metrics to Guide Changes:
- **Action:** Make informed decisions based on metrics such as click-through rates, conversion rates, and average time on listing. This data can help you refine your strategies effectively.

Encouragement for Ongoing Improvement:

Remember, the landscape of online selling is continuously evolving. The most successful sellers on eBay are those who remain curious, flexible, and proactive. Never settle for "good enough" when it comes to your listings. By embracing change and continually seeking to improve your strategies based on solid data and buyer feedback, you can sustain and grow your eBay business over time. Stay committed to learning and adapting, and view each change as an opportunity to optimize and thrive on eBay.

www.ingramcontent.com/pod-product-compliance
Lightning Source LLC
Chambersburg PA
CBHW050244230526
45470CB00005B/2104